The

Story of St. Frideswide,

Virgin and

Patroness of Oxford.

BY

FRANCIS GOLDIE, S.J.

C. Goldie.

Saint Frideswide escapes from Oxford.

Respectfully Dedicated

BY PERMISSION

TO HIS EMINENCE

JOHN HENRY NEWMAN,

CARDINAL-DEACON OF ST. GEORGE IN VELABRO, AND PRIEST OF THE
ORATORY OF ST. PHILIP

WITH THE CONVICTION

THAT

THE MEMORIES OF THE PATRONESS OF OXFORD

CANNOT BUT BE DEAR TO HIM.

PREFACE.

———

THE labours of the Bollandists have left little
to be done by a biographer of St. Frideswide.
In their exhaustive Life of the Saint, October,
vol. viii., they publish as their text the *Vita*
from the collection of John Capgrave, of which
a fine copy occurs in the Tanner MS. XV. in
the Bodleian Library. It is simply a transcript,
with some verbal alterations, and those but
few, of the Life given by John of Tynemouth in his *Sanctilogium*. Of this the MS.,
which is in the Cottonian Library at the
British Museum (Tiberius E. I.), is one of
those which suffered in the great fire of 1731.
All that remains of it has lately been restored.
The portion containing the Life of St. Frideswide (Art. 122, fol. 258–60) has suffered at
the top of each leaf only, the rest is distinct

and clear. John of Tynemouth wrote *circ.*
1366. A still earlier MS. of the thirteenth
century, probably even of the end of the
twelfth century, by an author whose name is
unknown, and whose work apparently escaped
the notice of the Bollandists, is preserved in
the Laudian MS. 114, formerly c. 94 in the
Bodleian. It is mentioned by Hardy in his
Catalogue of Materials, vol. i. part 1st.
p. 462. The narrative has evidently served as
the basis of John of Tynemouth's work, and
he has copied verbatim the words which the
anonymous author puts into the mouth of the
various speakers. The account given by this
writer is fuller and more consecutive than
that of his copyist, and leaves one under the
impression that Capgrave made bad use of
the materials before him. I have ventured
therefore to follow the Laudian MS., and cannot do better than give the prologue of its
author in full.

"I have collected into one volume, dearest
brethren, all I could learn about the Life and
virtues of the most blessed Virgin Frideswide

— so worthy of all veneration — either in chronicles, or in certain books of authentic histories, or in the catalogues * of English Saints. Therein it plainly appears that the author of the Life of that most holy Virgin, whoever he may be, was far from any error in many things, however contemptible he may seem to some supercilious critics who were led to blame him for his simplicity of style, and who thus proved that they cared more for beauty of flowers than for usefulness of fruit."

I have entitled my little work "The Story of St. Frideswide," that I might follow in the footsteps of the simple-hearted author, and so avoid critical examination of details. The main facts are shown by the Bollandists to be worthy of credit, and Holy Church has set the seal of her approval on the holiness of the glorious patroness of Oxford.

F. G.

Preston, 1880.

* "Catholicis" (*sic.*).

THE

STORY OF ST. FRIDESWIDE.

——◆——

THE upper waters of the river Thames flow through a broad and fertile valley. And just above the spot where the Cherwell adds its tribute to the greater stream, the river is broken up into many courses, girdling rich islets. Many times in the year the waters, swollen by the rains, rise over their banks, and for miles the country is like a lagoon.

In this place, when our story opens—then hardly known to fame—was a small town. It was seated on the north of the river Thames, and guarded on the other side by the swiftly flowing Cherwell. Had the Old Britons

chosen the site, protected as it was on almost
every side by marsh and stream ; or did their
conquerors, whose highroad passed not far
from it, plant their standard in the well-
watered valley ? History does not tell. But
when England was a Saxon land and ruled
by many kings, an eorlderman, or petty
prince, named Dida, was Lord of Oxenford.
This was in the early part of the eighth
century as nearly all chroniclers agree.* It
was a period of fierce wars between Mercian
and West Saxon kings; and though the
Christian faith which St. Augustine and his
successors had brought from Rome had
triumphed throughout the land, the old law-
lessness of the sons of Woden broke out again
amidst the clash and excitement of war. Dida
was, however, a good Catholic,† and his stain-

---

* See the list of authors and dates given in Boll.
† Laud. MS.

less life was an honour and an example to the town in which he lived. His lady was named Safrida. A happy pair, God blessed them with a girl, who was born to them in their home at Oxford. She was baptized without delay and called by the name of Frideswide. Her good parents took all pains to bring up carefully their child. And soon they saw what a treasure of wit and holiness Heaven had given to them. When she was five years old, a holy and learned lady, Algiva,* was charged with her education. So apt a pupil did the little Frideswide prove that in some five or seven months she learnt by heart the whole of David's Psalter. And as her mind opened

---

* Leland, *Collectanea*, London, 1774, vol. i. p. 279, quoting from a life of the saint by an author unknown, states in the margin, " Algiva perhaps was the abbess of Our Lady's at Winchester." Dugdale, however, states that this house was not founded till the reign of Alfred (vol. ii. p. 451). Capgrave says that Algiva was the saint's nurse, and had suckled her when a babe.

out beneath the teaching of Algiva, so the
love of her crucified Lord filled her soul,
and for His sake she courted suffering. She
afflicted her innocent body, ever girt with a
hair shirt; her only food was barley bread and
a few herbs; her only drink was water. She
sought upon her knees in prayer the face of
Him she loved. And dear to God, dear too
she was to all around her. No work was too
lowly or too poor for the nobly born maiden
to do for the poorest of the poor; no sorrow
which did not win her sympathy, no want
within her power to relieve which she did
not relieve.

While she was yet but young she lost her
mother. No wonder that, in rough times,
St. Frideswide sought for safer shelter. No
wonder that the love of an Eternal Spouse
had taken early possession of her heart.
Frideswide again and again gently urged her

father to make himself ready for the journey
on which her mother's soul had gone before.
And to send on to safe keeping for everlasting
life his earthly goods, she persuaded him to
build a church in honour of the Holy Trinity,
Our Lady, and all the Saints.

And then she begged a still greater favour,
that she might be allowed to dedicate herself
body and soul to God in this new sanctuary.
Dida bravely gave back to His Lord what His
Divine Master had given to him ; and he built
her a dwelling by the church where, with
twelve other ladies of gentle birth, she retired
from the world.   At the eorlderman's request,
the bishop of the diocese, Edgar of the see
of Lincoln, consecrated the thirteen virgins
in their new home.   Not content with his
first gifts, Dida endowed the church and convent with broad lands and farmsteads.

Living now for God alone, our saint gave

herself still more entirely to prayer and penance. Like the Apostle of Ireland, when all the world was at rest, a hundred times each night she bent her knee in worship of God. The enemy of our race envied both her peace on earth and the reward she was amassing for hereafter. He was too wise to tempt her directly to ill, but he took the old, old way of drawing her into evil under the seeming of good. He came to her in a vision of light, under the form of Her Divine Lord, with troops of shining angels around him, devils in disguise. " Come," said he to St. Frideswide; " come, my beloved, come; for the time has arrived for you to receive the crown that will never wither, of glory eternal,—a crown thou hast so well deserved. Come and prostrate adore my footprints, as long thou hast desired to do; for I have willed to appear to thee that thou mayest see me even in this passing life after whom thou hast sighed and art athirst with love, that so in transport of adoration thou mayest, without bodily pain, gain the joy of eternal life."

To him the maiden, taught by the Spirit of Truth, made answer: "Wretch! how canst thou promise to others what, because of thy pride, thou neither hast nor ever canst have? What has undying life to do with thee, who leadest ever a dying life, and liest for ever ruined and beneath the scourge? I too, wretched and miserable sinner that I am, would share with thee thy ruin, had not my Saviour Christ, whom thou pretendest to be, forestalled me by His mercy. For He has been my hope from youth." The proud demon could not bear such lowly words, and fled away with hideous howl and foul smell, leaving St. Frideswide calm and unmoved in the strength of her prayer.

Then her enemy tried a fresh means to ruin her. Her father was gone to his rest, dying of fever, after the building of the convent. The wicked Algar,* one of the great nobles of Mercia, like too many of the lawless princes of his day, a pagan in life if not in creed, had heard of or seen the pearl of Oxford. In his coarse breast the devil stirred up a brutal passion against the holy nun, which Algar concealed under the name of love. To gratify it he determined by stratagem, or, if not, by strength. And so, as he lived afar off,† he sent some of his nobles to lay

---

* Camden in his *Britannia*, vol. ii. p. 196, says, on the authority of Thomas Talbot, that at the period of St. Frideswide, in the reign of Ethelbald, King of the Mercians, in 716, Leofric was Earl of Leicester, to whom succeeded in direct line Algar I. and Algar II. King Ethelbald's character bears an unpleasant resemblance to that of Algar of our story. A MS. in the Bodleian calls Algar, King of Leicester. Hearne makes Dida a subject of Algar. The Bollandist writer of the saint's life hesitates to say who the tyrant might be. Capgrave states that Dida was living when his daughter returned from Abingdon.   † Laud. MS., p. 134.

before her an offer of marriage, with orders
that should she decline it they must carry
her off by force. They came to the convent
and laid before her their message. Strong in
God's strength, she gave them swiftly a calm
and courteous answer. "Had I thought of
marriage," she answered in a lowly voice, " I
would not have refused my lord Algar. But
as I now am wedded to Christ, the Everlasting
Lord, surely it would be dreadful, think you
not, to pass Him by, and take a man as short-
lived as myself?" * Then the embassage threw
off all reserve, and plainly threatened the
virgin with ruin worse than death. She

---

* We venture on a translation of the metrical version
Rawlinson MS., of this speech of the saint :—

> " 'Tis loathsome to desert the Heaven's King.
> I count as dung the favours promised me ;
> Nor can I wed, my Husband living still ;
> Nor to a lower king myself submit.
> Blameful would't be my first love to despise,
> Fool must he be, who asks the lowest first."

answered with St. Agnes : " You cannot stain my honour, if in my heart I withhold consent." Then as they rushed upon her to drag her from the holy place, with tears St. Frideswide called upon God Her Helper, and He struck her assailants blind, and so saved her from their hands. But the news got abroad, and the townspeople flocked in. When their first surprise was over, they begged the saint—perhaps it was from fear of Algar's wrath—to implore God to give back sight to the blind men. She prayed a Christian's prayer, and when they saw again, they flung themselves with changed hearts at her feet to beg pardon for their attempted crime, and then went home, to tell their lord the strange ending of their adventure.

The warning, however, was thrown away on the king, whom passion had made mad. He did not recognise the hand of God in what had happened, but put it down to charms and magic. He could not believe that any one was strong enough to oppose his will. In a fury of disappointed desire, he called for his horse, and rode off to Oxford.

St. Frideswide meantime, as was her wont, was spending the night in tranquil prayer, when, lo ! an angel came before her. " Knowest thou not," he said, " that to-morrow Earl Algar will be at the city gate ? He comes to satisfy his passion, if any way he can succeed. Fear not, for our Lord Jesus Christ will guard the sweet abode thou hast made for Him in thy spotless heart. The prince will return baffled and mocked, and punished with perpetual blindness. Hasten then down to the river side, and thou wilt find there a boat made ready for thee by God, and a guide, a steersman, for thy journey." Our saint thanked Her Lord for His protection, and, taking two sisters with her, hurried to the Thames. There she found a youth of heavenly look, clothed in dazzling white, who with words of comfort seated them in a boat, and in a short hour's space landed them some ten miles down the stream, near to where Abingdon now stands. No sooner were they on shore than boat and boatman vanished. A dense forest covered the country side, broken only by any clearing the monks of Abingdon might have effected around their infant monastery.* Near to Abingdon the saint and her companions found a path which led them into the fastnesses of the woods.

* The Laud. MS. and Capgrave called the place Benton, *i.e.* Benson or Bensington, where the Roman road, Akeman's Street, crossed the Thames. The metrical version gives Bampton as the site of the saint's retreat. But the Balliol MS. has Bendon, *i.e.*, Abingdon, which is nine miles and a half by the river, answering to the description of being ten miles from Oxford, while Bensington is more than twice that distance, and Bampton cannot be much less.

There the three fugitives sought shelter, and found it in a ruined building, the entrance to which was completely hidden by mantling ivy. It had been built as a cover for the herds of swine which roamed in search of acorns, and formed so large a source of revenue to the owners or tenants of the English forests.

Algar by this time had drawn near to Oxford, when he learned that his prey was gone. He made wild threats and offered large bribes to find her hiding-place. The townsfolk swore a solemn oath, they knew not where she was; still Algar vowed he would destroy the place, if she were not discovered. But as he rode towards the northern entrance to the town, he was stricken, as had been his messengers, with total blindness. The sudden visitation terrified Algar, but it wrought no change in his heart. Beaten and baffled, he returned home

as wicked as when he came.* The memory
of this event left so deep an impression, that
till the reign of Henry III. no monarch dared
to enter what became St. Frideswide's Church.†
Our saint spent three years in the deep soli-
tude of the forest, turning its glades into a
cloister of constant prayer, of fasting and
watching. God at last made known her holiness, and glorified her by a miracle. A
maiden of Abingdon of good birth had lost
her sight by the action, so it was supposed, of
an evil spirit. As she was asleep one night,
some one stood by her side and bade her go

* Mabillon in his *Ann. Benedict.* lib. xxi., xxxiii., says that
at St. Frideswide's prayer Algar regained his sight.

† Some writers say that no king entered Oxford, others that
none dared to pass the North Gate, the well-known Boc-
cardo by St. Michael's Church, whose early tower is so notice-
able an object in modern Cornmarket Street. Wikes in
his chronicle, A.D. 1275, says even Edward I., although his
father had ventured to go in, turned back from the city out
of fear of sharing the fate of Algar. The royal palace of
Beaumont stood outside the old walls.

to the dwelling-place of the saint in the wood. There she was to catch a drop of water as it fell from St. Frideswide's hands when washing, with it to bathe her eyes, and she was promised that she should regain her sight. As soon as day dawned the maiden told her parents, and they gladly led her to the spot. The saint, no doubt forewarned, allowed her to enter and take of the water, and straightway she saw. The girl and her friends quickly spread the news far and wide.

Fearing the perilous fame, St. Frideswide fled from the place. Taking a boat, she and her companions went up the river, past their convent of Oxford a mile or more, to a place belonging to her father called Binsey. She chose the spot, because near enough to her sisters to be able to give them the help of her guidance, and yet far enough off to be free from frequent visits. Other reasons, too, she had. She did not want to expose her community to fresh danger on her behalf; she wished to fly the notoriety she had gained by her victory over Algar. Her new home was not far from the convent of Wytham, which Cilla had founded, the sister of Hean, the first Abbot of Abingdon. When the Danes had destroyed this house, Catholic piety erected at no great distance from its site the well-known convent of Godstow.

Under pleasant uplands and not far from the river, with many sluggish water-courses crossing and recrossing the low ground around it, was a slight eminence called Thornbury, the Hill of Thorns; and herein amidst the thickets and fens, in what, when the floods are out, becomes an islet, our saint made a little oratory of osiers, covered roughly with planks, in honour of St. Margaret, the Virgin Martyr who had overcome the dragon. Hard by she

built herself a humble cell, and as there was a
lack of drinking-water, at her prayers a well
sprang up, which is there to this day.*

It chanced that a young man was needlessly
working on Sunday, cutting down wood, at the
neighbouring village of Suckworth.† Suddenly
the handle of his axe cleaved to his hand as
though it had been of red-hot iron. In vain
he tried to shake it off, he could not open his
fingers or let go his hold. His fearful screams
brought his parents and friends to the place.
They all proposed, as the sole resource, to seek
St. Frideswide's aid. So they crossed over the
river and reached her cell. There, with piteous
cries, the young man implored the saint to
take compassion on him, and his father and
mother joined him in his prayer. St. Frides-

* It has been lovingly restored of late years, and a respect-
ful inscription carved upon the arch above.

† *Sevecordia.* Laud. MS. Suckworth grew into a place of
importance owing to St. Frideswide's well. It is now no more.

wide's heart was touched, and asking God for help, she made the sign of the Cross on his hand ; the axe fell to the ground, and in a short while the wound was healed.

Another time some fishermen had cast their nets late at night, and while waiting to draw them in they fell asleep. In a sudden frenzy, one of them rushed at his comrade, and was going to tear him like a wild beast with teeth and hands. The others started up, amazed and horrified at what they took for a demoniacal possession. They succeeded in securing him, and with his hands tied behind his back they led him to Thornbury. Gently the saint made the saving sign over the raging man, and said : " I adjure thee, Satan, in the Name of the Great Son of the Living God, our Lord Jesus Christ, depart from this man, who is made to the image of God, nor dare any more to vex him." At these words the poor man fell to

the ground like a corpse.   But St. Frideswide
laid her hand upon him, and at her words:
" Man! arise in the Name of Jesus Christ of
Nazareth," straightway he arose in perfect
health and strength.

There is a legend which has taken some root
in France, that, to escape still more completely
from the notice of the world, when Cuthred
was King of Wessex, St. Frideswide secretly
fled across the seas with two companions to
Boulogne, intending to follow the example of
King Ini and so many Saxon princes, by mak-
ing a pilgrimage to the centre of Christendom.
Then—so the story runs—she stopped on her
way at a spot not far from Térouanne, where,
on the top of a hill crowned with wood, and
watered by a sparkling fountain, she stayed
some time.   But finding her new home was
too near the English shores, she went on by
Rheims, and then across the wild Alps to Rome,

where her virtue shone out so brightly—if the legend be true—that a church was built there in her honour. And when her devotion was satisfied, she came homewards, passing again through Artois to England.*

Be this as it may, the village of Bomy, near Boulogne—the place where Charles V. and François I. concluded a truce — still cherishes the memory of the Oxford saint under the name of St. Frewisse. Her chapel is on the hill-top hard by, and the stream still bears her name, " La fontaine de Sainte Frewisse," which it has borne for more than seven hundred years.†

* The Saxon chronicle says that in 737 Ferthere (Fort-here?), Bishop of Sherburne, went to Rome with Frithogith, the Queen of Essex. The Bollandists dismiss the legend of St. Frideswide's leaving England as without historical basis. Perhaps the name of Frithogith was confounded with that of our saint. Neither is there any record of a church dedicated to her in Rome.

† Desiderius, Bishop of Artois, as far back as 1187, speaks of this fountain as of a place held in veneration, v. Boll., Oct. 19, p. 561.

When at length the hour of St. Frideswide's reward drew near, she determined to return to her convent, to give back her soul to God in the place where first she had entered His service in religion. On her coming to Oxford the whole population turned out to welcome her. Amongst the crowd of priests and people that poured out to receive her, was a young man, whom leprosy had made so hideous that the chronicler says, he looked like a block rough hewn, out of which the hand of a sculptor was going to draw forth a human figure. His voice was almost gone, but as best he could, he murmured out the strange request : " I conjure thee, Maiden Frideswide, by the Almighty God, to kiss me in the Name of Jesus Christ, His Only Begotten Son." He bore about him the loathsome disease which then was deemed contagious, and never had the lips of man from earliest childhood come near her pure form. Yet to the amaze of all, on fire with charity, straightway she came up to him, and having first made over him the sign of the Cross, impressed a kiss on his offensive lips. In an instant the corrupt skin fell off in scales, and his flesh became bright and delicate as that of a little child. The whole town was full of the wonder, but the more she was praised all the more humbly did St. Frideswide chastise her body and her soul.

Soon after, when the measure of her merits was full, an angel again stood before her whilst at prayer and delivered her a message from God : " On the 14th of November, when the Sunday morning will break in on the night, your last end, Frideswide, is decreed, and you who despised the palace of your earthly father will enter the bridal chamber of the Eternal King, where is unfailing light, with life that knows not death." A very severe fever seized

upon our saint, and her strength began to fail.
As she lay on her bed she told those who were
sitting beside her : " Dig for me this day a
grave in the Church of the Most Blessed Mary
Ever Virgin, Mother of God and of my Lord
Jesus Christ, by whose aid I may more easily
despise the snares of the malignant spirits, and
may with greater surety stand before the judg-
ment-seat of the Son of Our Blessed Lady.
And when to-morrow the memory of His Re-
surrection will be kept, and I this very night,
after the third cock-crow, shall leave this passing world, I should not wish any one to be
wearied for me by digging on a feast so great
and solemn." Then she begged that the Blessed
Eucharist might be brought to her. And when
she had received it with thanksgiving, she kept
on blessing Her Lord. And as her eyes were
fixed on heaven, she beheld coming down towards her the two virgin saints whom she

had ever most specially venerated in life.
They came, and bowing reverently with joyful
accents, she exclaimed : " Welcome, blessed
saints! Oh how great is the multitude of Thy
sweetness which Thou hast hidden for them
that fear Thee, which Thou hast wrought for
them that hope in Thee! Who will not fear
Thee, O Lord, and magnify Thy Name, for
Thou alone art merciful? Lest Thy servant on
her way to Thee should be terrified at the on-
slaught of Satan, Thou hast sheltered the paths
of those who go forward. For, even when
beaten and confounded, is he wont to bring up
the falsehoods of his deceits against conquering
souls, as they are returning home to Thee from
the battlefields. Shelter us as Thou knowest
best. Thou hast granted, too, to me to behold
on my departure those sainted virgins, whom
Thou hast granted me of old to love during
my life, with a sort of familiar veneration.

From this it seems to be evident how Thou teachest Thy faithful to reverence with peculiar honour some one or another of those servants who, thanks to their merits, have gone to Thee."

The sisters by her bedside, startled at her loud words, asked her to whom she was speaking. "Do you not see," she answered, "those most holy virgins, SS. Catharine and Cicely,* are approaching?" And then, turning to them, she exclaimed, "Now I come, my ladies, now I come." And so, bidding good-bye to all around her, at the hour she had foretold, she departed to God. At the very same time a light from heaven lit up the place where lay her sacred remains and illuminated the whole town, while a rich fragrance of priceless perfume told that the Only Begotten Son of the Father of lights had been

* By a strange coincidence the figures of SS. Catharine and Cicely appear in the new stained glass in the north and south aisles of Christ Church.

there, whose Name, like ointment poured out, fills the whole world.

As a proof that St. Frideswide was living after death, a wealthy man, whose frame was paralysed and whose speech was gone, was brought in his servant's arms to the bier whereon she lay, and the moment he touched it he was healed, and leaping up with a loud voice told the praises of God and of our saint. And when, amidst a great throng, her holy remains were being borne to the grave, a man whose lower members were so contracted that he could only crawl along, with his hands resting on little stools, dragged himself as best he could to the funeral. But as he could not reach the bier, nor get into the church when the body was carried there because of the crowd, he did what remained to him, by crying out to the saint, as though she were still alive : "O maiden of priceless holiness, O spouse of the Fount of Mercy, how long I have been wishing to come to thee, but, wretched as I am, my ills of body and of soul have hindered my drawing near! Because of my sins it has not been granted me to see thee either alive or dead. Yet, lady, turn thy compassionate heart to me and heal me from this illness; for I believe for certain this is very easy for thee now that thou hast deserved to go to Him to whom nothing is impossible." His cry drew the eyes of all upon him, when on a sudden, with a loud crack, the contracted sinews became free and his legs became strong. Up he rose, and, free from all pain and full of joy, he took up his supports and pushing through the crowd, threw himself down at the saint's tomb, and, casting down there his supports, he thanked God and His glorious servant, St. Frideswide. So the sorrow of all was changed into gladness when it was seen what wonders God wrought through His servant after her death.

The body was laid in the Church of the Ever-Spotless Virgin Mary, the Mother of God, on the south side near the Thames.*

When Ethelred the Unready, to destroy the Danes who had taken refuge in the tower, set fire to the building, although the whole was burnt, her relics, which were then under ground, did not suffer. As a reparation for what he had done, the king rebuilt the church on a much larger scale. In consequence, the tomb of St. Frideswide, which till then had been on one side,† came to be in the centre of the church. How soon it took her name, which it bore for so many years, and how soon her spiritual daughters were dispersed, we do not know. The lava stream of Danish inva-

* *Prope*, Laud. MS. As what was St. Frideswide's is some way off the stream, *prope* must have meant *towards*.

† *In parte*, Laud. MS.

sion most probably broke up the community,
and their place was taken by secular canons.
Later on, when the Normans had conquered
England, no doubt the lands of the Church
had suffered in the troublous times, and but a
few clerics were left to minister at its altars
and in its choir.* Bishop Roger of Salisbury,†
chancellor of the realm, had become patron
and proprietor of the place, and handed it over
to the canons regular of St. Augustine, whose
active and zealous priors soon made it more
worthy of the patron saint of Oxford.

Near to the old church, or on its site, a
grand new church arose, in the solemn style
of the period which the Norman builders had
brought from Rome, a Christian adaptation
of the old traditions of the Imperial City—
sanctifying for God's worship what the genius

* Leland's *Collectanea*, vol. iv. p. 158.
† *Loc cit. :* "Cujus tunc, ut ego colligo, ditionis herus ille
fuit."

of the world's conquerors had created. Thus
we in England call it Norman, while in other
lands it goes by the name of Romanesque.
So earnestly had the first priors laboured that,
in the first year of his office, Philip of Crick-
lade, the third prior, was able to transport
the saint's relics into the new priory church
—the same which is now standing in Oxford
as the chapel of Christ-Church College and
the cathedral of Henry VIII.'s new diocese
of Oxford.*

King Henry I. had summoned around him
to his palace, outside the walls of Oxford, a

---

* Capgrave says, *v*. Boll., p. 565, 12, that the saint's relics were
first disinterred and placed in a shrine by a *vice-comes* called
William, the patron of the church. But when this took place,
or who this William was, he does not tell us, though it would
seem to refer to the time before the Conquest. The very early
Norman doorway leading to the chapter-house is thought to
have been the entrance to an earlier church than that built
by the canons regular, and perhaps it was a later addition to
the church of Ethelred. This may have been the scene of
what Capgrave narrates.

number of the bishops, clergy, and nobles of England, and the prior took the opportunity of their presence to translate the saint's remains, from the place where they had reposed for nearly 480 years, to the new shrine which he had prepared for their reception. The king, fearful no doubt of the fate of Algar, did not come. But at Prior Philip's invitation there were gathered at the priory on February 12, 1180, Richard the Archbishop of Canterbury, Galfrid Bishop of Ely, John Bishop of Norwich, and Peter Bishop of St. David's, to assist at the ceremony. And with them were John Scott the Archbishop-Elect of St. Andrew's, and one Master Alexius, a papal nuncio, who was on his way to the court of Scotland to support the claims of justice, and procure for John the mitre which his sovereign had denied him. A solemn fast had been kept, as was the custom, to prepare the august

assembly for the holy work ; and then, in the
midst of crowds of England's best and greatest
men, reverently and lovingly the tomb was
opened, and reverently and lovingly were the
remains of St. Frideswide borne into the new
church to their appointed place, a chapel on the
south side of the church.* A fragrant perfume
burst from the hallowed bones, and the "smell
of *their* ointments" was "above all spices."

But greater proofs of God's pleasure at His
virgin spouse were given, and these Prior Philip,
to the glory of the Giver, carefully recorded,†
himself in many cases an eyewitness of the
wonders wrought, in all cases wrought in his
own days, and mostly before the crowds that
flocked from every part to venerate the shrine

---

* Dugdale's *Monast.*, vol. ii. p. 141, note *a*. Probably the
south-choir aisle.

† The document was published for the first time by the
Bollandists, who pass upon the value of the evidence the
judgment given in these pages.

of the ever-popular Oxford saint. It would be
tedious to reproduce them all, but St. Frideswide's honour makes it a duty to speak of
some. Each is recorded with great care as to
the names of persons and places, with details
of the disease or accident for which cure was
sought and obtained. And though many
might not satisfy the rigid requirements of
a Roman Congregation of Rites, many there
are so recorded as to make doubt of the super-
natural agency impossible, save to those who
reject all miracles, or, in face of the clear
words of our Divine Lord, deny their existence
in later days. In the interesting pages of the
good prior we can almost see the crowds
surging in at the church doors, the sick, the
blind, the palsied lying around the shrine,
the rich and poor keeping together the night
watch there, in the firmness of their faith
waiting for the moving of the waters and

for the grace of healing which God was to grant as a reward for the virtues of His good and faithful handmaid. We seem to hear, while reading, the shouts of joy and hymns of praise as in presence of all the mist rolled back from the eyes, and strength flowed into the limbs, as hearing returned to the ears, or reason dawned once more upon the brain. The crutches, the bandages, the bonds are thrown aside, votive candles are lit; and the record is carefully penned of the new wonder which God has wrought.

The crowd was gathered from far and near, and many are the names of the villages from which they came, entered in Prior Philip's book, that are familiar to any who have lived in or about Oxford. Two blind beggar women from Eynsham, Jurkiva and Rilda, sisters, who could not stir without a guide, came on their way to seek a cure. When they drew near

to Oxford, Jurkiva, to her great joy, entirely
regained her sight, and hastened on to offer
her thanks at the saint's shrine. Her cure
gave confidence to Rilda, who spent the night
in tears and earnest prayer before the tomb.
And so next morning her petition was heard,
and the peasants of the old abbey town gave
positive evidence as to the previous blindness
and the completeness of the cure of their
country folk. The same day a Norman girl,
eighteen years old, from Pillardington, near
Evesham, who for ten years had lost the use
of her right side, was praying at the shrine
in great pain. In presence of the throng she
regained the use of her limbs, numb and stiff
though they still were through want of use.
Another woman named Maud, who had been
bed-ridden for half a year, was restored to
health, though she had lost all power in her
limbs.

Another time a young man was brought from Coleshill, a raving maniac, who filled the whole church with his cries, and so frightened the bystanders that the canons ordered him to be removed. One of them, however, sprinkled him with blessed water,* and at once the madman began to grow calm, and before the High Mass was over he was praying in quiet and with devotion. Nor did he afterwards show any signs of madness, though for eighteen months he had been a terror to his neighbours. On the same day a mother had brought her boy, a child of three years old, to St. Frideswide's. He had been ill since Christmas, nothing was left of him but skin and bone, and while she held him in her arms sure signs of death came over him. Her friends tried to cheer her. His father was

---

* Probably water blessed with a special blessing in honour of St. Frideswide, or hallowed by the touch of her relics, rather than ordinary blessed or holy water.

urged to go and get the cerecloth for his burial; but, strong in hope, the mother would not consent, and for three hours she wrestled in prayer, the tears streaming from her eyes. A canon happened to pass, and he forced a few drops of blessed water between the rigid jaws of the dying child. Life came back. In a little while he spoke, though in a whisper, then cried aloud, and showed by his animation that he was quite well again, and, as a further proof, he ate heartily of an apple.

So celebrated did the shrine become on account of the miracles wrought there, that the Metropolitan, Richard Archbishop of Canterbury, came to sing Pontifical High Mass in the church. Crowds assembled to assist and to receive his blessing, and as the bells began to ring for the service, Wlirva, a woman from Abingdon, who had been deaf for five years, recovered her hearing. The same day a woman from London, who had been blind for five years, on entering the church regained her sight, and walked unaided up to the shrine.

On the Whitsunday following, a blind girl of seventeen, from Northampton, received her sight under circumstances which leave no doubt as to the miraculous character of the cure. The shrine of St. Frideswide was that day borne in solemn procession round her church. As it passed by where the girl was standing, those near to her saw blood gush from her sightless eyes. This again happened while Mass was going on, and when it was over she had so far regained her sight as to be able to distinguish the white habits of the religious as they were leaving the choir. At Vespers her cheeks were again stained by tears of blood, accompanied, as before, with acute and pricking pain. Spite of her sufferings, she got to sleep that night, and awoke perfectly cured. Dom Roger, the Lord Abbot of Abingdon, chanced to be at Oxford, and having heard of what had occurred, to test the truth, he held up to her, before a number of people, a piece of money and asked her what it was. She told him at once. The completeness of the cure was proved in many ways, and some of the girl's relatives who were in Oxford gave evidence as to the facts.

Pilgrimages, like most other good things, may be abused, and one day, among a band that had come in from a distance, there was a woman who had sinned deeply on the way. She would seem to have made but light of her crime, but when with her party she reached St. Frideswide's, a sudden fear came over her, and though the others passed in, neither door nor entrance of any sort could she see, but all seemed to her alike unbroken wall.

She tried to follow the rest, but in vain.
She noticed that numbers were flocking round
to the north porch,* but on her going round
the wonder was repeated. She could not
enter in. Startled and terrified, the poor
woman remembered her crime, or rather
first felt its guilt, sought elsewhere for a
confessor, repented, and made her peace with
God. The priest encouraged her to have confidence, and bade her follow him, and so he
went before her to St. Frideswide's, and she
without difficulty made her way to the shrine.
A wonder akin to this happened the same day.
A young man from Gloucestershire, on his way
to St. James of Compostella, came into the
church and found it full of people in a state
of great excitement at the miracles which
were being wrought. As he was listening

* Of this no remains exist, any more than of the west door,
three bays of the nave having been destroyed by Cardinal
Wolsey when he took possession of the priory.

in wrapt attention to their story, during a
sudden crush, a thief came behind him and
cut away his purse, containing some five
shillings, and then made for the door. But
no way out could he find. He dashed up
against pillar and wall, and the people stared
at his strange behaviour. Meanwhile our
poor pilgrim having gone forward to the shrine
to make his humble offering, there for the
first time found out his loss. It was clear
that in such a crowd the recovery of his
money by human means was impossible, and
so he turned in his distress to St. Frideswide,
and begged her not to let him be a sufferer
because his devotion had led him to her
church. Then he went up and down begging
of all he met, that, if any one had found his
purse, they would let him have it again. But
all in vain, and he was going away in despair,
bemoaning aloud his sad fate, when the thief,

half stunned by the blows he had received, came to him, stretched out to him the purse, and made off amidst the crowd. The story was soon bruited about, and the strange behaviour of the runaway thief explained.

A young knight named Pantefot (*sic*),* a man of family and of large estates, was so completely paralysed on one side that he had lost all use of his left arm and leg. He chanced to pass through Oxford, and the fame of St. Frideswide's power made him resolve to watch before her tomb. There he spent a night without closing his eyes. He asked a young man to bathe his left hand with blessed water, and at once it broke out into perspiration, and without his perceiving it the arm regained strength. The next day he was so completely cured that

* Possibly Grimbald Pauncefoot of Gloucestershire, whose son Richard received from Henry III. the manor of Hasfield, four or five miles north of Gloucester. *V.* Atkyns, *Gloucestershire*, p. 460.

he was able to lift even heavy weights with the lately crippled arm. He told all around the great favour received, and called on them to join him in thanking God.

John, the hereditary constable of Chester,* had been ill for a long time ; his appetite was gone, and, though he had spent largely on medical advice, no good had come of it. He, too, heard of the wonders at our saint's shrine, and vowed to go on pilgrimage thither should he recover. He was cured, and went at once to make a public act of gratitude before the tomb of his benefactress.

Prior Philip, the chronicler of these miracles, was himself a sharer in them. He had been suffering very acutely from tertian ague, and,

---

* John, the sixth Baron of Halton, founder of the Cistercian house of Stanlow, which was afterwards transferred to Whalley, and became the well-known abbey of that place. The year after St. Frideswide's translation he was governor of Ireland. He died at Tyre, in the Holy Land, in 1191. *V.* Ormerod's *Cheshire*, vol. i. p. 509, *et sq.*

seeing how many rich and poor from far and near had received health through her inter- cession, he spent a whole night before the shrine without the symptom of an attack. Encouraged by his success he came a second night to ask for complete health, and never again up to the time that he was narrating did he suffer from his pertinacious foe.

We must claim our reader's patience if, for our saint's honour, we tell of two more miracles, and then we shall have closed the selection. Agnes, a lady of good family, wife of Ivo, a goldsmith at Leicester, had lost her mind in consequence of a severe attack of fever. A number of people who had been on pilgrimage to St. Frideswide's chanced to stay at the goldsmith's house on their way home, and naturally were full of what they had seen and heard. The poor woman listened and understood, and made a vow to go herself.

Then and there her reason came back, and she too went to announce before the shrine the favours of God's right hand.

The brother of one of the canons regular of the priory, Benedict Repherin, a worthy gentleman of Oxford, had a little boy of five years old, called Lawrence, who had been a sufferer from infancy, and the doctors agreed there was no chance for his life save a painful and dangerous operation. A surgeon was called in, a handsome fee was paid, and more was promised if he were successful. Though he had the name of being skilful, he was unequal to the task, and only undertook it out of greed. The parents did not dare to witness the operation, and left their child in his hands. Poor Lawrence died under the knife. Terrified at what had happened, the surgeon went away, saying to the relatives of the boy that he had forgotten some ointments which he had left at home, and forbidding any one to go in till he returned. The mother waited for him in vain, and at last, after he had been away for two hours, she entered the room. The child lay strapped down to the operator's table. She called it, but it neither answered nor stirred. What was her horror to find it cut and slashed by the bungling operator. Half mad with grief, she sent for her husband, showed him the sad sight, and implored him to promise God that if, out of His mercy and for St. Frideswide's sake, He would but restore life to their child, they would dedicate it to their virgin patroness. And He, who through His prophet gave back life to the son of the Sunamite woman, heard the earnest prayer of these believing parents. As they knelt beside the corpse in strong supplication, the child opened first one eye and then another, as if awakening from sleep.

Then drawing up his little limbs, he yawned, and began to cry for his mother to bring him some food. When he was completely himself again, his mother asked him where he had been to, and what he had seen. He told her that a most beautiful lady had come to him, and made a great sign of the Cross over his body, and then disappeared. Benedict and his wife were weeping for joy, and they poured forth their thanks to God. They fulfilled their promise by dedicating the child to religious life, and by having him brought up for the altar.

Among the multitudes who came to venerate St. Frideswide was Henry III., the very first English sovereign who had ventured to enter the church. It was in 1246, on the Saturday before Passion Sunday, "the day," as Wikes the chronicler observes, "on which the whole Church throughout the world begins to sing the 'Vexilla Regis prodeunt.'"* With the sovereign came his brother, Richard, King of the Romans, and his eldest son, afterwards Edward I., who with a number of knights had been present at a parliament at Oxford. Henry left, as a proof of his devotion, an endowment for a priest to say a Mass every day in the church, and an annual revenue to keep four wax lights burning day and night around the shrine.†

From the time of the translation, it was the custom, twice a year, for the chancellor and scholars, the representatives of the university, to go in procession with the parochial clergy and inhabitants of the town to St. Frideswide's, where the chancellor delivered a sermon.

When the beautiful Early English chapel of Our Lady was built, alongside the northern

---

* The hymn for Passion-tide, which is sung at the first Vespers of Passion Sunday, on the Saturday evening.

† Dugdale's *Monast.*, vol. ii. p. 149.

choir aisle a splendid basement of stone, like
that of St. Alban's, was erected * to receive
the shrine of St. Frideswide. The old shrine,
then much time-eaten and worn, was placed
within a new and more splendid feretory, and
on the Saturday within the octave of Our
Lady's Nativity, September 10, 1289, it was
solemnly translated by the prior, Robert de
Ewelme. William de la Corner, Bishop of
Salisbury, assisted, perhaps invited in recog-
nition of the benefaction of his predecessor to
the canons regular. Edmund, Earl of Corn-
wall, and a great multitude of clergy, secular
and regular, were present.

The vaulting over where the shrine stood
was richly decorated, like that over the tomb

---

* Compare the description of St. Thomas' shrine in Dean
Stanley's *Memoirs of Canterbury*, London, 1865, p. 228. "The
lower part of the shrine was of stone. The shrine, properly
so called, rested on these arches (p. 229), blazing with gold
and jewels, the wooden sides plated with gold."

of St. Francis at Assisi, some traces of which
now remain. A beautiful tomb, which is probably that of the good prior who built the
chapel, is still standing, and looks as though
he had chosen his place of sepulture near the
spot where reposed the body of the virgin
saint, whom he had loved to honour in life.
A noble lady, Elizabeth Montacute, who had
endowed the Lady Chapel with half of what
is now Christ Church Meadow, was buried
at his feet, under the rich polychrome monument so familiar to any who visit the cathedral of Oxford.

A formal announcement was made to the
Convocation of the Province of Canterbury,
held in 1481 at St. Paul's, London, that the
Sovereign Pontiff had lately raised to the
altars SS. Osmund, Frideswide, and Etheldreda.
This was, no doubt, in answer to the petition
of the English clergy who, as was the custom,

had doubtless applied to the Holy See for a formal sanction of the *cultus* already paid to these servants of God. It was many years later before the modern procedure of canonisation became the rule. In consequence of this Papal decree, the Convocation ordered the feast of St. Frideswide to be kept throughout England with an office of nine lessons. This is to be found in the Sarum Breviary, but it is worthy of note that the lessons of the second nocturn—generally containing the Life of the saint of the day—are merely of the Common of a Virgin not a Martyr. Whether this arose from any doubt of the authenticity of the details of her life, or from what other cause, we cannot say. The Collect, Secret, and Postcommunion are, however, *proper.**

* COLL.—Omnipotens, sempiterne Deus ; auctor virtutis et amator virginitatis : da nobis quæsumus Sanctæ Fredes-

Almighty and Eternal God, source of truth and lover of virginity, grant us, we beseech Thee, that the merits of St.

Towards the close of the fifteenth century a handsome tomb, in the late Perpendicular of the period, was erected between the monument of Lady Montacute and the east wall of the

widæ virginis tuæ placitis tibi meritis commendari, cujus vita merito castitatis tibi complacuit. Per Dominum, &c.

Frideswide, Thy virgin so pleasing to Thee, may be as a commendation of us to Thee, whose life by its chastity gave to Thee such satisfaction. Through Our Lord, &c.

Secr.—Offerimus tibi, Domine, preces et munera in honorem Sanctæ Fredeswidæ virginis tuæ gaudentes; præsta quæsumus ut et convenienter hæc agere, et remedium sempiternum valeamus acquirere. Per Dominum, &c.

To Thee, O Lord, we offer with joy prayers and gifts in honour of St. Frideswide : grant us, we beseech Thee, fitly to do this, and to gain an eternal reward. Through Our Lord, &c.

Postcom.—Prosint nobis, Domine, quæsumus sumpta mysteria, pariterque nos, intercedente beata virgine tua Fredeswida, et a peccatis exuant, et præsidiis tuæ propitiationis attollant. Per Dominum, &c.

May the mysteries we have received benefit us, and may they, through the prayers of the Blessed Virgin St. Frideswide, likewise strip us of sin, and uplift us by the protection of Thy mercy. Through Our Lord, &c.

—Sarum Missal. Antwerp: 1527. *Oct.* 19.

Lady Chapel.   All memory of those whose names it was intended to perpetuate is gone, like the brass which once adorned it.   The matrix shows the form of a man and a woman. Popular tradition called this the tomb of St. Frideswide, and believed that the two figures had represented Dida and Safrida.   Over it was erected an oaken chamber, in the same style as the monument, evidently for the purpose of keeping watch over the shrine exposed night and day, with its precious jewels, to the crowds which flocked around it.   This till lately was thought to have contained St. Frideswide's body.

One of the very last of the long and illustrious roll of pilgrims to the shrine of St. Frideswide was poor Catharine of Aragon, who came early in 1518, attended by Cardinal Wolsey, to pay her devotion at the virgin's tomb.   But a very few years later, Pope Clement VII. made over

the church and priory to the cardinal for a
college of secular students. Before he could
carry out his magnificent scheme, the jealousy
of his capricious master cast him down from
the high position to which he had raised him,
and Henry VIII. seized the new college and
its belongings. A terrible change was come,
and in 1539 the shrine, with the precious trea-
sures with which Catholic piety had adorned it,
was rifled, and the spoil swept into the royal
coffers. The relics of the saint seem to have
escaped destruction, and were once more honoured during the brief sunshine of faith in
Queen Mary's reign. On the change of religion
under Elizabeth, they were hidden away in some
remote part of the church. The Royal Com-
missioners in the preceding reign had ordered
the body of an apostate French nun—the first
woman ever admitted into an Oxford college,
the scandalous partner of the apostate canon

regular, Peter Vermigli (Pietro Martire)—to
be exhumed from her tomb close to St. Frideswide, and buried beneath a dung-heap in the
Dean's stables. This was in accordance with
law ecclesiastical, if not civil, of the time,
when churches were considered holy, and when
the unbaptized or public sinners could find no
burial in consecrated soil. The zeal of the new
Protestant subdean, one Calfhill, made him dig
up her body, and, with a refinement of irreve-
rence under the cloak of respect, sought for
and found the relics of St. Frideswide, to
mingle her remains with those of the fallen
nun. The relics were discovered in two silken
bags, worn with age and the devout lips of
thousands of reverent Catholics. For this sacrilegious proceeding a solemn service was held,
and after a violent sermon from the subdean,
in which abuse of the saint were mingled with
praises of Catharine Dampmartin, the *çi-de-*

vant nun, their bones were laid together in the tomb of the saint.*

Soon the Sacrifice was again forbidden, and the old chant silenced once more. Still the memory of the good patroness was not altogether forgotten. High above the reach of sacrilegious hands her statue has stood in its niche in the tower, looking down sadly on the ruthless changes all around her.

She saw the blanched head of brave Mr. Nappier, who had given his life for their common faith, upon the college gate, and the mangled remains of other sufferers for the same cause. For a moment, under an unwise but well-meaning king, she witnessed the revival of the great Sacrifice in more than one of the colleges around her church. But for a

* This tomb was possibly where her relics were buried after the destruction of her shrine, though Sanders, *De Schismate Anglic.*, lib. iii., p. 293, speaks of it as "antiquissimum monumentum."

moment, and then things were darker than before. Strange changes have there been since then. And now, after three centuries of neglect, a loving hand has written on brass the memory of the place where once the saint's relics were honoured, and where they have lain so long forgotten.

In piam memoriam Beatæ Frideswidæ

Quæ decursu sæculi post Christum natum VIII

   Vetustissimum hic cœnobium

Constituit Fundatrix regebat Abatissa

Reliquiæ ejus A.D. 1180 e sepulchro

In hanc ecclesiam tum nuper ædificatam

Solemniter translatæ

Deinde A.D. 1289 in novum feretrum

Hic ipso in loco extructum depositæ

Tandem subtus conditæ sunt.

Fructus justitiæ in pace seminatur facientibus pacem.

Hanc tabellam ponendam curavit W. B. Canonicus.

In loving memory of Blessed Frideswide,

Who, in the course of the eighth century after Christ,

Of this most ancient monastery
Was the foundress and abbess.
Her relics in 1180 from their tomb
Were solemnly translated
Into this church, then but lately built.
Again, in 1289, they were placed in a new shrine
Erected on this very spot.
Finally they were buried here beneath.
The fruit of justice is sown in peace, to them that make
    peace.
This brass was laid down by the orders of Canon W. B.

May her memory once more become glorious in the city which once gloried in her
name. May her mass and office once more,
at least at Oxford, take its place in the
Church's Calendar. And may young men and
maidens try to emulate, in days of self-indul-
gence, St. Frideswide's love of God and her
fear of sin and stain.

16667786R00036

Printed in Great Britain
by Amazon